HANDBOOK FOR
NEW EMPLOYEES

HANDBOOK FOR
NEW EMPLOYEES

"To truly master your fears you must become
the monster that lurks in the unknown and embrace
the abyss."

~ West Brimstone CEO & Founder of PEPTFIM Co.

FIRST EDITION
2014

Table of Contents

Your First Day
PEPTFIM Facts That Murder
Welcome to Hell
Your First Month
What to Work On
Why do I need to pick my own projects?, But how do I decide which things to
work on? How do I find out what projects are under way?, Short-term vs. long term
goals, What about all the things that I'm not getting done?, How does
Peptfim decide what to work on? Can I be included the next time Peptfim is
deciding to hire person X?
Teams, Hours, and the Office
Cabals, Team leaders, Organic Structure happens, Hours, The office
Risks, What if I screw up?, But what if we ALL screw up? Will I Die?
Your Peers and Your Performance
Peer reviews, Pyramid ranking (and compensation)
Your First Six Months
Roles, Advancement vs. growth, Putting more tools in your toolbox
Hiring, Why is hiring well so important at Peptfim?, How do we choose
the right people to hire?, We value "+ shaped" people, We're looking
for people stronger than ourselves, Hiring is fundamentally the same
across all disciplines.
What Is Peptfim *Not* Good At?
What Happens When All This Stuff Doesn't Work? Will People Die
Where Will You Take Us? Where Will We Take Mankind?

First edition: April 2014
PEPTFIM Company
Spokane, Washington USA
www.peptfim.com
Designed by PEPTFIM Co.
Typeface: ITC New Baskerville
10 9 8 7 6 5 4 3 2 1

Preface

In 2006, we set out to conquer the known free world, but we knew back then that we had to first create a business model that was designed to foster true greatness and individuality. We first had to create a place where incredibly talented and driven "fellow travelers" are empowered to produce and distribute their best "work" into the minds and hearts of billons of unsuspecting sheeple, with very little to stand in their way. If you are reading this you have been carefully selected to take part in this ever growing cultural revolution that will change the very face of mankind forever.

This book is an abbreviated encapsulation of our guiding principles. As PEPTFIM Co. continues to grow, we hope that these principles will serve each new recruit joining our ranks. If you are new to PEPTFIM, welcome. Although the goals in this book are important, it's really your ideas, talent, greed and life force magic that will keep PEPTFIM thriving in the years ahead. Thanks for being here. Now let's have some bloody adventures together shall we?

How to Use This Book

Here at PEPTFIM Company we carefully scout out the greatest leaders and innovators from around the world to help us achieve our goals and spread our message. Even if you're just starting out now, you'll have many opportunities to rise up into a leadership position by proving your own greatness in every task you accomplish. This book demonstrates our major ideas and values along with simple guidelines that will help you on your way. Read through its pages and apply its principles into every job your given and you'll be successful.

WELCOME TO PEPTFIM

Your First Day

So you've gone through the long interview process, you've
signed the contracts in blood, spoken the sacred vowels, and you're
finally here at PEPTFIM COMPANY.
Congratulations, and welcome.
PEPTFIM has an incredibly "unorthodox" way of doing things
that will make this the greatest most fulfilling professional experience of
your life, but it can take some getting used to and be confusing at first.
This book was written by people who've been where you are
Now, and who want to make your first few months here
as easy and with as few injuries and fatalities as possible.

Peptfim Facts That Murder

Peptifm is 100 % self-funded.
Without pressure from outside entities such as
corporations and governments we are free to advance
our own agenda and the truth as we see it fully uninhibited.

Peptfim owns its intellectual property.
At PEPTFIM we champion true freedom of thought.
We bow down to no government. No idea that seeks to
enslave, pacify, control or otherwise oppress humanity
in any way. With that in mind we understand the dark nature
of mankind without the rose colored glasses. There are rules and
ways to survive and even thrive in this merciless
and sometimes hopeless world.

Peptfim is more than your average company.
The very meaning of Peptfim exemplifies what we believe in
and remains indistinguishable from man's long and tattered history.
"PEPTFIM" ; *People Eat People The Future Is Murder.*
With this in mind we at PEPTFIM offer a new way of thinking
and a better way of living as a result of excepting the harsh realities.
Man was made to suffer and the second you accept this fact your reality
becomes more bearable and in turn manageable. Through this we reject
the old system and we strive to make our own through self determination
and strength to overcome all.
No bullshit. Harsh truth. Amazing products. A new way of living and thinking.

Welcome to Hell

At PEPTFIM you will be tested and tried. We will push you and sometimes shove you into achieving your full potential. We don't play nice because we don't have to. We hire APEX hunters and reject the victim mentality that has slowed and diminished the progress and integrity of mankind. We don't suffer fools here. That starts with not hiring any. The second step is accurate job placement. If you're not right for the job we simply move you to another to help bring out your own personal niche.
The world has become Hell. The people who hold power and perpetuate the great lie that you have no power have made it this way. It's your job to sell it back to them. This is your revenge.

Company Structure

Here at PEPTFIM we use a form of Hierarchy that is similar to the animal kingdom
which is great for maintaining strength and ferocity as one company unit?
It simplifies planning and makes it easier to function as a large group of people from the top down.

 How does it work? Simple, the most intelligent person with the most successful ideas is not going
to be delivering coffee or running copies such as an adult lion who is the leader of a pride in the wild
does not sit around and wait to be feed. He leads his pride with his own physical strength and
ingenuity. As exemplified by the lion you are expected to lead and contribute to this company with
your own strengths and creative ingenuity.

PEPTFIM CEO

Upper Management & Peptfim Share Holders

Lower Management

Team Leaders

Peptfim New Hires

Third Party Contractors, Field Agents,

Project Company CEOs & Paid Off Politicians/ Government Officials & Lobbyists.

Moving Up The Food Chain

We expect you to want to rise up and take out someone weaker and less deserving of the job than you but ONLY if it is shown through continual demonstration and agreed upon by the company CEO. If in agreement by upper management you and the other employee will both receive a notice to switch positions. The employee being supplanted will be shown his missteps through collected evidence of his own failures by supporting upper management. In the case of an upper management position being supplanted that person will be handled directly by the CEO. As part of our founding values and company structure you as employees by choosing to work of PEPTFIM Co. accept and understand that it is important and necessary for the survival of the company to operate in this way.

The Customer

Every company will tell you that "the customer is boss," but
Here at PEPTFIM that statement means something a little different.
The customer does in fact deserve the best product we can and will produce.
At Peptfim company we do understand that there are scammers and manipulators out there
along with competitors in disguise who only want to use you for the destruction of the company and
capture of its trade secrets and other valuable information. Knowing the difference between these
types can be crucial for maintaining your own employment and the survival of the company.
There's no red tape stopping you from figuring out for yourself what our clients
want, and then giving it to them. There's also no red tape for you to use and "dispose" of the
competition and parasites who only seek to do the same to you. Don't waste your time debating this
universal fact and understand that it is a cut throat world. "People Eat People." If you're thinking to
yourself, "Wow that sounds like a lot of responsibility" you're right. And that's why hiring new
talent is the single most important thing you will ever do at PEPTFIM. We need employees who can
perform these tasks without hesitation.
(see "Hiring ," on page 42).

Any time you interview a potential hire, you need to ask yourself not only if they're talented or
cunning but also if they're capable of literally running this company, because someday they will be.

Why does your chair have a trap door underneath? Yes , you read that correctly. This is not a joke fuck face. The contract you signed when you started working here gives us the legal loophole.

Think of the trap door as a symbolic reminder that you should always be considering where you could end up if you drag the company down through your own personal weakness and stupidity. Here at PEPTFIM we do not believe in a long drawn out firing process. People usually know for a long while why they are being fired before that day actually comes.

You'll notice people moving frequently; people will often prefer to walk around the office instead of sitting. We find that this increases productivity and makes for a more in shape employee.

Where do the trap doors lead? Not knowing is half the fun and if you really knew you probably wouldn't have the balls to continue working here, again separating the wheat from the chaff. We only want people who have no fear of failure. If you have questions and need help please find your supervisor on the company office map located on each floor near the restrooms.

Settling in

Your First Month at Peptfim

So you've decided to stick it out. You can preform
your job with some competency now.
You've had some time to study the inner workings and have
already made some friends and hopefully some enemies.
Good ! Time to outwit your rivals and push yourself
further ahead. It's very rare that any employee at PEPTFIM
stays in the same position through his/her entire employment
with us. Thanks for showing up every day on time with your
eye on the prize. This next section walks you through figuring
out what to work on. You'll learn about how projects work,
how cabals work, clandestine meetings and how products
get created here at PEPTFIM.

What Do I Work On?

Why do I need to pick my own projects?

First , you shouldn't even be asking that question.
Stop sitting around waiting for someone to tell you
What to do ! Make your own work. How can you generate
New income streams for the company ? That is the
only question that should always be on your mind.
With the support of PEPTFIM behind you the world is
at your fingertips. If you have a new idea and if that idea needs
company funding fill out a F627 form and deliver it to
management. This process may take several days. No new
idea gets funded without direct approval by the CEO.
If we like your idea or need more information you will
be contacted. If you receive a disproval notice simply
move onto the next idea or find a way to fund it yourself.
Believe in your ideas and you will always find a way.
We've heard that other companies have people allocate a
percentage of their time to self-directed projects.
At PEPTFIM, that percentage is 100.

How to Choose a Project- Continued.

Since PEPTFIM is run by an animal hierarchal business model, people don't join projects because they're told to, They join projects to prove themselves and move up the food chain. Whoever brings in the most revenue will surely move up into a higher position.

The best projects which require more than one employee are ones in which people can see demonstrated value; they staff up quickly. The idea founder of that particular project ultimately decides the best most fitting team of employees to man the job , keeping in mind the failure or success of the project rests upon his/her shoulders. Trust is eventually formed between employees and project sabotage for personal advancement is met with swift "termination" which will be determined by upper management. If you're working here, that means you're good at your job. People are going to want you to work with them on their projects, and they'll try hard to get you to do so. But the decision is going to be up to you. If you feel like you're already working on something bigger and better do your own thing. The important part is using your own intuition to determine the best ideas and with one's are worth exploring.

How do I decide which things to work on?

Deciding what to work on can be the hardest part of your
job at PEPTFIM. This is because, as you've found out by now,
you were not hired to fill a specific job description. You
were hired to constantly be looking around for the most
valuable and lucrative work you could be doing.
At the end of a project, you may end up well outside what
you thought was your core area of expertise.
There's no rule book for choosing a project or task at
Peptfim. But it's useful to answer questions like these:
• Of all the projects currently under way, what's the
most valuable thing I can be working on?
• Which project will have the highest direct impact
on society? How much will the work I ship affect the average man?
• Is Peptfim not doing something as a whole that it should be doing?
• What's never been done before? What's the most rewarding? What leverages
my individual strengths the most? How can I infiltrate government and religious
organizations to further the PEPTFIM agenda ? How can PEPTFIM consolidate
power between its project companies? How can I use my own business or
personal contacts to help me complete my project ?

Settling in - Continued

How do I find out what projects are under way?

New approved projects are posted on the screens in
the center of each floor's office work space and also
added to the PEPTFIM internal company website for
sign up and review. If in doubt just ask around.

Short-term vs. long-term goals

At PEPTFIM we are all responsible for prioritizing our own
work, and because we are conscientious and anxious to be
the best, as individuals we tend to gravitate toward projects
that have a high, measurable, and predictable return for
the company. So when there's a clear opportunity on the
table to succeed at a near-term business goal with a clear
return, we all want to take it. Do it. And, when we're faced with a
problem or a threat that is not the competition, scammer or other
outside parasite, and it's one with a clear cost, it's hard
not to destroy it immediately. *WAIT AND REPORT !*
If an employee is a clear threat
to the company you must produce that evidence of this to
upper management. If the threat is upper management you must
report it directly to the CEO discretely and immediately as these
tend to be the greatest threats to the company itself.
Our lack of a traditional structure comes with an
important responsibility. It's up to all of us to spend effort
focusing on what we think the long-term goals of the company
should be.

Someone told me to (or not to) work on X. And they've been here a long time!

Well that person is obviously trying to fuck you over.
They want the project for themselves or want you to join a shitty project that's not going anywhere. They are more than likely will be getting the trap door soon and want you to be sucked down with them. Ignore their psychological games and use your own discernment to figure out which projects are worth working on and which people are worth working with.

Whatever group you're in, whether you're building Micro startup companies for new income streams for PEPTFIM , working on consolidating existing project companies into a more functional conglomerate type system for Peptfim or bribing government and or FDA officials . It's crucial that you believe in what you're doing so we'll repeat our values a few more times in this book to further instill our core belief system.

What about all the things that I'm not getting done?
It's natural in this kind of environment to constantly feel
like you're failing because you probably are.
For every one project you decide to work on, there will
be dozens that aren't getting your attention. Trust us,
this is normal. We only expect you to devote time to the
best opportunities that come your way.
It is critical that you to learn how to choose the most
important work to do with the greatest impact on society.

How does Peptfim decide what to work on?
The same way we make other decisions: Occult magic!
Combined with advanced methods of meditation,
Sacrifice rituals , remote viewing and intuition we have perfected
a system for choosing new ideas. By actually seeing into the
future we can steer the ship that is humanity on the correct course.

Seeking Out New Talent

Recruiting can be a difficult process to instrument and
Measure at first. Although we have always tried to be highly
logical about how we hire new Peptfim employees, we've
found much room for improvement in our approach over the
 years. We have made significant strides toward bringing
more predictability, measurement, and analysis to recruiting.
A process that many assume must be treated as highly
unpredictable due to the stresses of the job and the
cut throat atmosphere. Hiring the right employee has to do
with personality traits, body language, basic intelligence
and subtle nuances. There of course is a science to it.

Can I be included the next time Peptfim is deciding PERSON X?

No. Unless it's your own project and you are hiring a third party private contractor. Leave the official
PEPTFIM hiring to us we know what we are doing. We hired you didn't we ? Hiring is reserved for
upper management. You cannot suggest your friends and family no matter how great you think they
are. Again if you have a better way; demonstrate how your idea is better than the current system and
prove it to us.

Cabals

With the PEPTFIM Company, a "CABAL" usually constitutes a small group of project
Companies that have come together in secret to influence and or eradicate
the competition. These monopolies are strictly off the official PEPTFIM books.
A simple example of this would be a small clothing company under a different name such as
HORRORpop LLC that is launching a new product. The launch of the new product is crucial to the
survivability of HORRORpop LLC and in turn an important income stream to PEPTFIM as a whole.
How can you use PEPTFIM as a whole to discretely tip the odds of success in your favor ? You
would then seek out another PEPTFIM media/news company to block the competitor's ads that day
and run your own media ads instead. We have a number of paid off CPSC officials who can and will
streamline your approval status and deny our competitors' products whether it is through fake
complaints or accusations of lead poisoning.

Project Leaders

If the project was your idea, you are the "lead" for a project.
This person's role is not a traditional managerial one as that
right is only held by Peptfim upper management team and can be
taken away from you at any time we see necessary.
Most often, the leaders for the projects act as primarily
a clearinghouse of information.
They're keeping the whole project in their head at
once so that people can use them as a resource to check
decisions against. The leads serve the team, while acting
as idea centers for the entire project.

Structure happens

Project teams often have an internal structure that forms
temporarily to suit the group's needs. Although people at
PEPTFIM don't have fixed job descriptions or limitations on
the scope of their responsibility, they can and often do
have clarity around the definition of their "job" on any
given day. They, along with their peers, effectively create a
job description that fits the project goals. That description

changes as requirements change, but the temporary structure
provides a shared understanding of what to expect
from each other. If someone moves to a different group or
a team shifts its priorities, each person can take on a completely
different role according to the new requirements.
PEPTFIM lets you make all the organizational decisions
about your group's structure. Although it may step in and
redirect the project temporarily but that is very rare.

Most problems show up when group hierarchy or codified divisions of
labor either haven't been created by the group's members or when
those structures persist for long periods of time after the project
is completed. We believe those structures inevitably begin to serve
their own needs rather than those of Peptfim and its customers. The
hierarchy will begin to reinforce its own structure by using the in-office
selection process described earlier and finding people who fit the projects
shape, adding people to fill subordinate support roles.
Its members are also incented to engage in rent-seeking behaviors
that take advantage of the power structure while focusing on
delivering the highest value to our customers. These two things must
always be kept in mind.

Hours
While people at other companies occasionally choose to push themselves to
work some extra hours at times when something big is
going out the door, Here at PEPTFIM its expected! You'll never get ahead
working fewer hours than the next guy. Again you are in charge of your own
projects and micro companies. You ultimately decide your level of participation.
You control how far you go or don't go.

A Brief Timeline of PEPTFIM's History

2006 Peptfim Co. is formed in Spokane, WA,
by West Brimstone.

2006 – Formation papers are signed.
Peptfim starts off as a small independent publishing
Company. Brimstone starts selling his original paintings
with covert PEPTFIM indoctrination imagery.

2007 - Brimstone receives some of his first worldwide press
bringing the PEPTFIM message to the world stage.

First gallery shows and the small front company ;
West Brim Studios is created during this time.
West Brim Studios LLC is involved in the creation of
Several small clothing companies during this time.

2008 - More shows and publications during this time.
West Brimstone writes his first book ; "Fighting For Fiction."
Peptfim expands into toys and other household
products during this time.

2009 - Peptfim expands business locations to Portland Oregon.
Peptfim Co. creates its first cartoons and music videos.
West writes his second book ; "Nonsense Relevant" along
with a full length graphic novel reviling the inner workings
and business model entitled ; "Dead Business Men."
Several more project clothing companies are created
during this time with the more popular designs sold to
major manufacturing companies.

2010 - Peptfim Co. begins to produce music under its own production
label signing in new artists. An inner marketing/research company
is created.

2011 - Peptfim begins to diversify and consolidate power reaching into
Other markets such as oil , pharmaceuticals , 3d printing
and military technologies. Peptfim receives its first government project.

2012 - Peptfim begins to corner the mass media market through
several front companies and television news channels.
Peptfim's CEO West Brimstone writes his third book entitled ;
"BITTER BATTER BRAINS."
This in fact is a secret Peptfim code book for future projects.
Peptfim at this time invests in water purification technologies. At this time the
first PEPTFIM lobbyists take up permanent residencies in Washington DC.

2013 - Further company conglomeration continues. PEPTFIM becomes highly
Invested in private space technologies.

2014 - Peptfim establishes several Hollywood production houses and alternative
media outlets, controlling both the mainstream and the alternative information markets.
The PEPTFIM religious and political parties are created.
Peptfim now controls over 100 sub-companies and employees
over 50,000 full time employees.

The office

Sometimes things around the office can seem a little too good to be true. If you see someone walking down the hall one morning twirling a machete smoking a marijuana cigarette while wearing last month's dirty laundry while heading into one of our private Asian massage rooms, don't freak out. All these things are here for you to actually use. And don't worry that somebody's going to judge you for taking advantage of it—relax! And if you stop on the way back from your happy ending massage to play on the gun range or work out in the PEPTFIM 24 hour gym or whatever, it's not a sign that this place is going to come crumbling down like some 1999-era dot-com startup. These things are here for you and PEPTFIM is too big to fail.

Risks

What if I screw up?

Yes we reserve the right to fire you at PEPTFIM for making a mistake
And by mistake we mean a direct action/decision on your part that
loses us money.
It wouldn't make sense for us to operate any other bullshit
politically correct way. Employees that make us money are
rewarded handsomely and the ones that don't deserve no mercy.

Providing the freedom to fail is an important trait of the company
Which emphasizes total freedom of though and champions
individuality and originality. We couldn't expect so much of
individuals if we didn't penalize people for errors.
Expensive mistakes, or ones which result in a very public failure
, are genuinely looked at as a betrayal of the company itself. Screw
up on your own time, not ours. We hired you because you are the elite
and we expect perfection every time.
Never be afraid to run an experiment or to collect more data.
It helps to make predictions and anticipate nasty outcomes.
Ask yourself "what would I expect to see if I'm
right?" Ask yourself "what would I expect to see if I'm
wrong?" Then ask yourself "what do I see?" If something
totally unexpected happens, try to figure out why. Don't play
the blame game. Take responsibility.

But what if we ALL screw up?

We Don't !

So if every employee is autonomously making his or her own decisions, how is that not chaos? How does Peptfim make sure that the company is heading in the right direction? When everyone is sharing the steering wheel of their own project company,

Over time, we have learned that our collective ability to meet challenges, take advantage of opportunity, and respond to threats is far greater when the responsibility for doing so is distributed as widely as possible. Namely, to every individual at the company.

We are all stewards of our long-term relationship with our customers. They watch us, sometimes very publicly.

Methods to find out what's going on

step 1. Talk to someone in a meeting

step 2. Talk to your floor supervisor.

step 3. Search the news section in the company's internal website.

step 4. Talk to one of the many whores in the massage room.

PART 3
How am I doing?

Annual pyramid ranking (and compensation)

At Peptfim we preform an evaluation annually to rank each other against our peers. Unlike peer reviews, which generate information for each individual, pyramid ranking is done in order to gain insight into who's providing the most value at the company and to thereby adjust each person's compensation to be commensurate with his or her actual value.

Peptfim pays people very well compared to industry norms. Our profitability per employee is higher than that of Google or Apple or Microsoft, and we believe strongly that the right thing to do is pay our best employees the most.

Your Peers and Your Performance

We have two formalized methods of evaluating each other: peer reviews and pyramid ranking. Peer reviews are done in order to give each other useful feedback on how to best grow as individual contributors. Pyramid ranking is done primarily as a method of adjusting compensation. Both processes are driven by information gathered from each other.

Peer reviews

We all need feedback about our performance in order
to improve, and in order to know we're not failing. Once
a year we all give each other feedback about our work.
Outside of these formalized peer reviews, the expectation
is that we'll just pull feedback from those around
us whenever we need to.

There is a framework for how we give this feedback to
each other. A set of people (the set changes each time)
interviews everyone in the whole company, asking who
each person has worked with since the last round of peer
reviews and how the experience of working with each
person was. The purpose of the feedback is to provide
people with information that will help them grow. That
means that the best quality feedback is directive. Here at
Peptfim we understand that your fellow employees will
sometimes try to give you shitty reviews. That's okay,
We look at how much revenue you bring in annually to
the company making a kind of checks and balance system
for determining if you're a real asset to the company or not.

How am I doing?

Compensation

Peptfim does not win if you're paid less than the value you create.
And people who work here ultimately don't win if they get
paid more than the value they create. How much meat have
you offered up to the beast that is Peptfim ? How much should
you take home after all is said and done?
So Peptfim's goal is to get your compensation to be "correct."
We tend to be very flexible when new employees are
joining the company, listening to their salary requirements
and doing what we can for them. Over time, compensation
gets adjusted to fit an employee's internal peer-driven
valuation and total revenue generation. Not just for the year but
your total revenue generation since you've started at Peptfim.

That's what we mean by "correct"—paying someone
what they're worth (as best we can tell using the opinions
of peers and our total worker revenue generation data reports.
The removal of bias is of the utmost importance to Peptfim Co. in
this process. We believe that our peers are some of the best judges
of our value as individuals but your worker revenue data is the best
judge of your value & compensation overall.
Our business structure eliminates some of the unfounded bias
that would be present in a unanimous peer-ranking system elsewhere.
The design of our pyramid-ranking process is meant to eliminate as
much as error as possible.

If you think your compensation isn't right for the work you do, then
you should raise the issue. At Peptfim, these conversations are surprisingly
easy and straightforward. Adjustments to compensation usually occur
within the process described here. But talking about it is always the
right thing if there's any issue. Fretting about your level of compensation
without any outside information about how it got set is expensive
for you and for Peptfim.

Simple Method to working without a boss
step 1. Come up with an idea never before thought of
step 2. Tell a coworker about it and form a project team if needed
step 3. Work on it together to completion forming cabals if need be to achieve success
step 4. Ship it/Publish it/Produce it!

Compensation - Continued.

Each project/product group is asked to rank its own
members. (People are not asked to rank themselves, so we
split groups into parts, and then each part ranks people
other than themselves.) The ranking itself is based on the
following four metrics:

1. Skill Level/Technical Ability

How difficult and valuable are the kinds of problems
you solve? How important/critical of a problem can you
be given? Are you uniquely capable (in the company?
industry?) of solving a certain class of problem, delivering
a certain type of art asset, contributing to design,
writing, or music, etc.?

2. Productivity/Output

How much shippable (not necessarily shipped to outside
customers), valuable, finished work did you get done?
By choosing these categories and basing the pyramid ranking
System on them, the company is explicitly stating, "This is what
is true valuable." We think that these four categories offer a broad
range of ways you can contribute value to the company.
Once the intra-group ranking is done, the information
gets pooled to be company-wide. We won't go into that
methodology here which is covered in the upper management
employee handbook.

3. Group Contribution

How much do you contribute to studio process, tired party hiring, integrating people into the team, improving workflow, pushing your colleagues to excel, or writing tools used by others? Generally, being a group contributor means that you are making a tradeoff versus an individual contribution. Stepping up and acting in a leadership role can be good for your group contribution score, but being a leader does not impart or guarantee a higher stack rank. It is just a role that people adopt from time to time but keep in mind we are watching your total worker pyramid revenue reports or TWPRR's so don't fuck around. Being a team player can only take you so far.

4. Product Contribution

How much do you contribute at a larger scope than your core skill? How much of your work matters to the product? How much did you influence correct prioritization of work or resource trade-offs by others? Are you good at predicting how customers are going to react to decisions we're making? We hired you because you are already a self-starter and a true creator. Don't let us down.

Vacation

step 1. Think about where you want to go.

step 2. Toss the idea right out of your skull.

step 3. We have an Asian massage room in the office.

step 4. Work is your vacation. Love what you do and it won't be work.

Fig. 3-3 Method to taking the company trip

1. Fill out a VACC2 form and deliver it to upper management for approval.

3. Upon approval wait for the funds to appear in your business debit card account before leaving.

2. Make sure you are back in the office upon return on time.

4. Hand in your VACC3 business report along with any usable contacts made and contracts signed.

PART 4

DISCRETION

Undercover agents who interact with others outside the company call themselves
by various titles because doing so makes it easier to get their jobs done and continue working
covertly. Do not distribute this handbook or expose any of PEPTFIM's methodology to anyone
including your friends and family. If it happens we will be forced to pursue legal action including
liquidation of all your private assets and of course immediate termination.
Inside the company though we all take on the role that suits the work in front of us.
Everyone is a manager. Everyone can question each other's work. Anyone can recruit
someone onto his or her project including third party contractors. Again it's important to note, Third
party contractors are not employees at PEPTFIM Co. and are purposely *"kept out of the loop"* so to
speak. Do not give them information beyond what is needed to complete their tasks. What they don't
know won't hurt them.

Everyone has to function as a "strategist," which really means
figuring out how to do what's right for Peptfim and our clients around the world.
We all engage in manipulation, corruption, Magic and our own core intelligence that makes us the
elite and the masters of our own reality. Without these we would just be another slave who is forever
unaware that he is actually a modern day slave, searching for that promised end of the rat maze that
has and always will elude him . For them the future is murder. For us the future is what we are
creating for ourselves today.

Advancement vs. growth

Because Peptfim doesn't have a traditional hierarchical
structure, it can be confusing to figure out how Peptfim fits
into your career plans. Here is just one example ; John say's ;"Before Peptfim, I was an assistant
animation director in Hollywood. I was working my way up to becoming a director until the
economy dropped out so I quit and was quickly recruited by a Peptfim agent and was hired on here
but now that things are getting better with the economy how am I supposed to keep moving forward
here with my dream of becoming a director available to me again?"

Working at Peptfim provides an opportunity for extremely efficient and, in many cases, a very
accelerated, career path. If you choose to step down as an official employee at Peptfim with our
many production studios, movie houses and other broad ranging companies we control or own we
can simply hire you on as undercover agent / contractor and put you into a director position or other
leadership role in pretty much any company as long as you follow our guidelines and further our
agenda in which ever movie or projects you choose to work on for the duration of your career.

Your First Six Months

You've mastered the basics. Now you're moving
beyond wanting to just be a productive day to day employee.
You're ready to help shape your future, and Peptfim's. Your own
professional development and Peptfim's growth are both now
under your control. Here are some thoughts on steering
both toward success.

Roles

By now it's obvious that roles at Peptfim are fluid. Traditionally
at Peptfim, nobody has an actual title only team titles.
This is by design, to remove organizational constraints.
Instead we have things we call ourselves, for convenience.

Moving Forward

Most people who fit well at Peptfim will be better positioned
after their time spent here than they could
have been if they'd spent their time pretty much
anywhere else. You create successful companies
and control the people who run them for you. To pretty
much anyone else on the planet running just one successful company
alone would be a great accomplishment but it's what you do
on a yearly and sometimes monthly basis.
Work hard and keep pushing the boundaries
and you will get noticed. Our company's leadership isn't run by
millionaires but billionaires and they have all earned their spot starting
from the bottom and so can you.

Putting more tools in your toolbox

The most successful people at Peptfim are both (1) highly
skilled at a broad set of things , (2) world-class experts
within a more narrow discipline and (3) advanced practitioners of magic.
Because of the talent diversity here at Peptfim, it's often easier to become
stronger at things that aren't your core skill set.
We will push you to your full potential.

Creating new companies is only the beginning

If you were hired as a base level Peptfim employee,
you're now surrounded by a multidisciplinary group of
experts in all kinds of fields, creative, legal, financial,
even psychological.
Many of these people are probably sitting in the same room
as you every day, so the opportunities for learning are huge.
Creating new companies year after year forces you into
becoming modern jack of all trades.
Take advantage of this fact whenever possible: the more
you can learn about the mechanics, vocabulary, and analysis
within other disciplines, the more valuable you become as a leader.

PART 5

Peptfim is growing

We do not have an annual growth goal per say. We don't want you to
just continue to add new companies to our roaster without researching
what we already have. Find out what we don't have and make it. Ex;
We're not looking to own a hundred clothing companies, we only need
a few amazing , successful and trend setting clothes companies.
We will continue to hire the best people as fast as we can, and to
Continue scaling up our business as fast as we can, given our existing
staff. Fortunately, we don't have to make growth decisions
based on any external pressures, only our own business
goals. And we're always free to temper those goals with the
long-term vision for our success as a company. Ultimately,
we win by keeping the hiring bar very high.

Hiring

Success Starts Here

Many people ask what is our secret and
How is Peptfim so successful. I mean we can't
explain it all away with black magic but in fact it's a
direct consequence of hiring great, accomplished, capable people.
Getting this to work right is a tricky proposition, though, and depends
highly on our continued vigilance in recruiting/hiring.
If we start adding people to the company who aren't as
capable as we are at operating as high-powered, self-directed,
senior decision makers, then lots of the stuff
discussed in this book will stop working and people will get shit canned
and whole corporations and currencies will implode. We don't want that
do we ? Not unless it benefits us directly.
One thing that's changing as we grow is that we're not
great at disseminating information to everyone anymore.
On the positive side, our profitability per employee is
going up, so by that measure, we're certainly scaling correctly.
Our rate of hiring growth hovered between 11 and 19
percent per year, for years. In 2011, we sped up, but only to
about 20 percent per year. 2011 kept up this new pace,
largely due being able to hire more highly skilled individuals
who are already on top in their career fields.

Peptfim is growing - Continued.

When we bring in a great person we create value across the whole
company. Missing out on hiring that great person is likely
the most expensive kind of mistake we can make.
Usually, it's immediately obvious whether or not we've
done a great job hiring someone. A poor hiring decision
can cause lots of damage, and can sometimes go unchecked
for too long. Ultimately, people who cause damage always
get weeded out, but the harm they do can still be significant.

How do we choose the right people to hire?

An exhaustive how-to on hiring would be a Peptfim handbook of
its own.. It'd be tough for us to capture because we feel like
we're constantly learning really important things about how
we hire new people. In the meantime,
here are some questions we always ask ourselves when
evaluating candidates:

• Would I want this person to be my boss?
• Would I learn a significant amount from him or her?
• What if this person went to work for our competition?
• Can this person keep secrets ?
• Is this person a follower or a true leader?

Across the board, we value highly independent self-driven people.
That means people who are skilled in all the things that might advance
our company to new heights.
Hiring well is the most important thing in the universe.
Nothing else even comes close. It's more important than fucking and if
you suck at that you should probably be looking for a new job soon.
So when you're working on hiring—participating in
an interview loop or innovating in the general area of
recruiting.
When you're new to Peptfim, it's super valuable to apply what you've
had to go through in your own interview process and use that same
system in evaluating people you are going to hire to help create and
run your future project companies.

Why is hiring well so important at Peptfim?

At Peptfim, adding individuals to the organization can influence
our success far more than it does at other companies either in a
positive or negative direction.

===
===

Peptfim is growing

We're looking for people stronger than ourselves.
When unchecked, people have a tendency to hire others
who are lower-powered than themselves. The questions
listed above are designed to help ensure that we don't
start hiring people who are useful but not as powerful
as we are. We should hire people more capable than
ourselves, not less. Ask yourself ; Could this person
beat me at a game of chess or decapitate me in a mortal
combat grudge match type of situation ?
In some ways, hiring lower-powered people is a natural
response to having so much work to get done. In these
conditions, hiring someone who is at least capable seems
(in the short term) to be smarter than not hiring anyone at
all. But that's actually a huge mistake.
This is why we'll often pass on candidates
who, narrowly defined, are the "best" at their chosen
discipline.
Of course it's not quite enough to say that a candidate
should collaborate well—we also refer to the same four
metrics that we rely on when evaluating each other to evaluate
potential employees
We scout out and recruit "+ - shaped" people.
That is, people who are both generalists (highly skilled at
a broad set of valuable things—the top of the +) and also
experts (among the best in their field within a narrow discipline ,
the vertical leg of the +).
This recipe is important for success at Peptfim. We often
have to pass on people who are very strong generalists without
expertise, or vice versa. An expert who is too narrow has
difficulty collaborating. A generalist who doesn't go deep
enough in a single area ends up on the margins, not really
contributing as an individual. It's like falling in love, if we
just aren't feeling "it" , if there is no intuitive connection
in the interview process then we will follow our instincts
and we just won't hire that person.

Peptfim is growing – Continued.

Q: If all this stuff has worked well for us, why doesn't every company work this way?

A: Well, because it's really hard. From day one, it requires a commitment to hiring in a way that's very different from the way most companies hire. It also requires the discipline to make the design of the company more important than any one short-term business goal. And it requires a great deal of freedom from outside pressure—being self-funded was key. And having a founder who was confident enough to build this kind of place is rare, indeed.

Another reason that it's hard to run a company this way is that it requires vigilance. It's a one-way trip if the core values change, and maintaining them requires the full commitment of everyone, especially those who've been here the longest. For "senior" people at most companies, accumulating more power and/or money over time happens by adopting a more traditional hierarchical culture. Here at Peptfim any senior member can be knocked off by any other employee that can do his/her job better at any time. People work hard for their spot in the team.

Q: What's the usual project completion time from start to finish?

A: Every project is different and requires its own unique timeframe for completion but over the years we have found that most projects are completed within the 3 to 8 month range.

Q: What happens during tax time ?

A: New employees are first put on a 1099 form status. This is your initial trial period. After your three month trial we put you on a standard W2. Upper management employees are salary based. See the upper management employee handbook for more information if this applies to you.

Q: What's with all these electric PEPTFIM company cars in the parking lot, and how do I get one ?

A: Once you reach a management position at Peptfim Co. it is standard practice to receive an official Peptfim company car. Upon ownership it is your responsibility to care for and maintain your vehicle. Each car is equipped with hidden infrared cameras and microphones for your protection. Park anywhere in the lower lot. The upper lot is reserved for upper management.

Hiring – Continued.

We sometimes hire on temporary/contract help to get
us through tough spots, but we should never lower the
hiring bar. The other reason people start to hire "downhill"
is a political one. We do perform several multidisciplinary
background checks on new employees. If you're hiring
outside help for your project company we expect you to
do the same. The number one reason for this is to stop our
competitors and outside government officials from infiltrating
our ranks which can damage the company and saddle yourself
with a broken organization. Be Smart!

Hiring is fundamentally the same across all disciplines.
There are not different sets of rules or criteria for hiring lobbyists,
engineers, artists, assassins, and accountants. Some details are
different - like, artists and writers show us some of their
work before coming in for an interview and assassins list their
past kills. We judge them by their criminal record, their high
profile hits and their professionalism under extreme pressure.
But the actual interview process is fundamentally the same no
matter who we're talking to.

"With the bar this high, would I be hired today?" That's
a good question. The answer might be no, but that's actually
amazing for us, and we should all celebrate if it's true
because it means we're growing correctly. As long as you're
continuing to be valuable and bringing in new revenue
streams, it's a moot point, really.

PART 6

Epilogue

What Happens When All This Stuff Doesn't Work? Will People Die ?

Sometimes, the philosophy and methods outlined in this book don't match perfectly with how things are going day to day. But we're confident that even when problems persist for a while, Peptfim roots them out, along with any person trying to undermine our interests.

As you see it, are there areas of the company in which the ideals in this book are realized more fully than others? What should we do about that? Are those differences a good thing? What would you change? This handbook describes the goals we believe in. If you find yourself in a group or project that you feel isn't meeting these goals, be an agent of change. Help bring the group around. Talk about these goals with the team and/or others.

What Is Peptfim *Not* Good At?

The intense cut throat design of the company has some downsides.
We usually think they're worth the cost, but it's worth noting that
there are a number of things we wish we
were better at:
· Helping new people push themselves harder. We wrote this
book to help but a book can only go so far.
· Mentoring people. Not just helping new people figure
things out, but proactively helping people to grow
in areas where they need help is something we're
organizationally not great at. Peer reviews help, but
they can only go so far. You are already at the top in
your career field and have your own connections.
Use them. We give you the freedom to expand and
grow here because like any real apex predator we know
you can't be caged.
· Disseminating information internally among upper
Management employees. We are working to become
more unified as a single company unit.
· Finding and hiring people in completely new
disciplines (e.g., economists! industrial bankers!).
· Making predictions longer than a few decades out.
magic can only go so far, the rest is up to us.
· Communicating with our abroad undercover intelligence assists.
· We miss out on hiring talented people who prefer to work within
a more traditional structure. Again, this comes with the territory
and isn't something we should change, but it's worth recognizing
as a self-imposed limitation but on the other hand let the other
guys have all the weak people that couldn't make it here.
You are the hunters and the real soothsayers. It is your job
to shape society behind the scenes. Remember our goals
and stay vigilant.

Glossary
Code words not already covered in the book & Peptfim Lingo

PCFM— Peptfim Controlled Federal Marshal

Empty Suit— Peptfim Controlled Political Figure.

AWPRR— Annual Worker Pyramid Revenue Report

CMEET— Calling together Several Peptfim controlled
     organizations for a Cabal.

PFASH— A Peptfim safe house for overseas agents.

PEPTFIM— People Eat People The Future Is Murder

PPC— Peptfim Project Company.

CCKS— Country Currency Kill Switch

PPR— Potential Peptfim Recruit

SCTMM— Social Change Through Media Manipulation.

RFBP— Religious Fear Based Programming

PDW— A person that has a Peptfim placed death warrant out on them.
    The term also referees to a Peptfim Death Warrant in general.

PRUNNER— The assassin that actually carries out the hit on the designated PDW.

PRMM— Peptfim Ritual Magic Meeting.

HANDSHAKE— Referrers to a Peptfim bribe given to an elected or other government official.

REPOTTING— Is a term referring to the process of supplanting a higher up individual and trading
      Jobs at Peptfim.

PPFM— Referrers to the Peptfim philosophy of the future is murder for those that don't create their own.

PEP— Referrers to the Peptfim philosophy and undeniable truths of mankind's true dark nature
   of eating his fellow man to get ahead.

PFRDS— People within Peptfim Company who are assigned to destroy all financial records upon federal intrusion.

PFC— Peptfim Front Company.

PPCSM— Peptfim Project Company Start Money.

The Future

Peptfim will be a new company a few decades from now
because you are going to change it for the better. We can't
wait to see where you take us. The products, features, and
social change that you decide to create for the worlds
population are the things that will define us.
Whether it's a new way of communicating, a new vaccine,
a way to save Peptfim money, a painting that redefines what is
beautiful, something that protects us from legal threats,
a new military application, an idea for how to be healthier while we
work, a new mind control tool for Peptfim's multinational media
conglomerates, a spectacular blowjob, a new kind of A.I. that lets
our robots be learn faster, a flight controller that can take over the
controls of any aircraft from the ground or (more likely) something
nobody's thought of yet, we can't wait to see what kind
of future you choose to build at Peptfim.

www.ingramcontent.com/pod-product-compliance
Lightning Source LLC
Chambersburg PA
CBHW051822170526
45167CB00005B/2118